Stephen Perkins

Report on the pension systems and invalid hospitals of France,

Prussia, Austria, Russia, and Italy

Stephen Perkins

Report on the pension systems and invalid hospitals of France, Prussia, Austria, Russia, and Italy

ISBN/EAN: 9783743438163

Printed in Europe, USA, Canada, Australia, Japan

Cover: Foto ©ninafisch / pixelio.de

Manufactured and distributed by brebook publishing software
(www.brebook.com)

Stephen Perkins

Report on the pension systems and invalid hospitals of France,

Prussia, Austria, Russia, and Italy

SANITARY COMMISSION,
No. 67.

REPORT

ON THE

PENSION SYSTEMS,

AND

INVALID HOSPITALS

OF

FRANCE, PRUSSIA, AUSTRIA, RUSSIA AND ITALY,

WITH SOME SUGGESTIONS UPON THE BEST MEANS OF DISPOSING OF
OUR DISABLED SOLDIERS.

BY STEPHEN H. PERKINS.

NOTE.

The attention of the Sanitary Commission has been for a long while directed to the subject of a timely provision for the soldiers disabled in the war, after peace shall be restored. The question is full of difficulties. Very little inform-ation or guidance is to be obtained from books. The Commission learning, during the past summer, that Mr. S. G. Perkins, of Boston, was about visiting Europe, and being acquainted with his interest in similar questions, resolved to avail itself, if possible, of his talents and opportunities to collect information, by personal visits, or otherwise, touching the administration of Invalid Hos-pitals, and the provision made for disabled soldiers, in Europe. Mr Perkins accepted the appointment, and sailed soon after for France, where his investi-gations began. The annexed Report presented by him, embodies the results of his observations in the various countries which he visited. It will be found of interest to philanthropists and economists, and will also furnish us with valuable practical suggestions to guide our legislation, in its ultimate disposition of the future of our disabled soldiers.

NEW YORK, *July 1st*, 1863.

LETTER OF INSTRUCTIONS.

New York, August 15th, 1862.

Stephen G. Perkins, Esq.:

Dear Sir,—The Sanitary Commission are much exercised with the subject of the future of the disabled soldiers of this war. They calculate that, if it continue a year longer, not less than a hundred thousand men, of impaired vigor, maimed, or broken in body and spirit, will be thrown on the country. Add to this a tide of another hundred thousand men, demoralized for civil life by military habits, and it is easy to see what a trial to the order, industry, and security of society, and what a burden to its already strained resources, there is in store for us. It is, in our judgment, to the last degree important to begin now, to create a public opinion which shall conduce to, or compel the adoption of, the wisest policy on the part of our municipal and town governments, in respect of disabled soldiers—so as to discourage all favor to mendicity—all allowance to any exceptional license to those who have been soldiers—all disposition for invalids to throw themselves, any further than is necessary, on the support and protection of society. You, who have paid so much attention to social science, know how easily loose, indulgent and destructive notions creep into communities, under the name and purpose of humanity, and what temptations of a sentimental kind there will be, to favor a policy which will undermine self-respect, self-support, and the true American pride of personal independence.

In view of this, the Sanitary Commission is now studying the general subject of the proper method of dealing with our disabled soldiers at the close of the war, and, as far as possible, prior to that. The few guiding principles thus far excogitated, appear to be these :

1. As little outside interference with natural laws and self-help as possible.

2. As much moral and other encouragement and strengthening of the natural reliances as possible.

3. The utmost endeavor to promote the healthy absorption of the invalid class into the homes, and into the ordinary industry of the country.

In opposition to these principles will be the rivalry and competition of States, in generosity to disabled soldiers—similar to that which has appeared in running bounties to recruits up to an excessive and injurious height; the attempt to make political capital out of the sympathy of the public with the invalids of the war—issuing in over-legislation and over action—with much bad and demoralizing sentimentality—and, worst of all, a public disposition to treat this whole class as a class with a right to be idle, or to beg, or to claim exemption from the ordinary rules of life.

To illustrate what I mean by interference with natural laws, I should regard any general scheme for herding the invalids of the war into State or National Institutions, as a most dangerous blow to domestic order, to the sacredness of home affections and responsibilities, as well as a weakening of what may be termed the law of local sympathy. Their natural kindred are the first protectors of our invalids ; the local community, the next ; and the State the last. We must exhaust the two first before drawing on the last ; or, rather, we must cherish and sustain the two first by every possible means before resorting to the last, which in the end will require to be heavily drawn

upon. This is not a matter of mere pecuniary consideration.
It is not to save the State or National Treasury, but to encour-
age and save the spirit of independence, to preserve the self-
respect, and the homely graces and virtues of the People on
which all the real dignity and strength of the Nation rest.

To accomplish this result—*i. e.*, to restore the large proportion of all our invalids to their homes, there to live and labor
according to their strength, sustained and blessed by their own
kindred—we must have a sound, a generous, a wisely considered
pension law; and this pension law must be rid of all humiliat-
ing or enslaving character. It must be considered as the payment of what has been earned, and its payment should be made
regular, punctual, immediate, and with as little loss by agen-
cies and obstructions as possible. Moreover, the right to a
pension should not rest exclusively on visible wounds. Broken
constitutions, or impaired vigor, traceable unmistakably to military service, should entitle to a pension.

To employ to the utmost the law of local sympathy, the disabled and invalid soldiers should be encouraged in every way
to settle in the neighborhoods from which they came, and be
thrown as much as possible on the fraternal responsibility of
their neighbors for employment and sympathetic aid. A sense
of local or communal responsibility to leave the light employments in every village or hamlet to these invalids, should be
cherished. The emulations of towns could be depended upon
for this, were a proper start given to it by a judicious amount
of writing on the subject in the leading journals. In London,
by some recent law, one-legged or one-armed men have some
special privileges, as ticket-takers, parcel-bearers, messengers,
&c. (I hope you will find out when abroad precisely what it
is.) I am confident that if we begin right we can induce a most
extensive and most wholesome re-absorption of the invalids of
the war into the civil life of the nation, to the actual advantage

of its affections, its patriotism, and its honest pride. But the subject will need careful guidance.

After every thing has been done to discover and appropriate all light forms of industry throughout the whole circle of trades suited to maimed and invalid men, there will still remain those whom the small support of a pension, eked out by home protection or local sympathy and co-operation, will not adequately care for. The large body of foreigners, the reckless and unrelated, those who have hitherto been afloat, with such as are most seriously disabled, or have least natural force to provide for themselves—these must be collected in National Institutions. We don't want a vast net-work of soldiers' poor-houses scattered through the land, in which these brave fellows will languish away dull and wretched lives. Nor do we want petty State asylums, to be quarrelled about and made the subject of party politics. We want to economize our battered heroes, and take care of them in such a way as to maintain the military spirit and the national pride; to nurse the memories of the war, and to keep in the eye of the Nation the price of its liberties. After reducing to the smallest number this class, to be kept in the hands of the State, how best to deal with it is the chief problem connected with this topic; and the principal sources of light are, first, general principles, and next, the experience of other nations—for we have had next to none in our own country.

Of the general principles, a few occur to me at once:

1. Justice and policy both demand that these Institutions should be National, and not State Institutions. A war against State pretensions should not end without strengthening in every way Federal influence. This war is a struggle for *National* existence. We have found a *National* heart, and life, and body. Now, let us cherish it. I know that desperate efforts will be made to build up State asylums for these invalids. Let us judiciously discourage the idea from the start.

2. The Institutions should honor both military and civil life.
They should be military in their organization, control, dress,
drill, and maintain the antecedents of the war from which they
spring. The care of the trophies, arms, cannon, &c., might be
assigned to them. They should be made nurseries of our military glory, and should, in some way, be skillfully co-ordinated
with the popular heart, so as to feel, and to animate, the
national sentiment. At the same time they should be industrial—encouraging and allowing such an amount and variety
of labor as would discourage listlessness and monotony, and
prevent the feeling of utter dependence.

How these institutions are to grow up, is doubtful; whether
by degrees, as a necessity, or by bold legislation from the start.

We have thought, as a Commission, of asking the Government for the control and care of disabled soldiers from the time
they leave the Hospital as patients, and begin their convales-
cence, to the period when they are finally discharged; say four
months on the average; then to create special Hospitals (with
Government funds) for these convalescents, of a temporary character; to find out the homes, and favor the establishment in
their own local communities of all able to be thus provided for;
having an eye, through our village affiliated associations, to
their well-being and future career, and aiding in every way the
success of the just principles laid down in the earlier part of
this letter.

Then, retaining, partly at our own expense, (that is, out of
the spontaneous bestowments of the people,) all those disabled
men who are the proper subjects for permanent asylums,
finally to inaugurate a great asylum, with branches, partly
under our own control and management, partly under that of
the Government, which by degrees should embrace and embody
every wise, humane, and patriotic idea suited to the case.
Our dependence for success in such a scheme—very crude as

9

yet—would be the possession of more and earlier thought, better and fuller information, a profounder and wiser plan— such a plan as would recommend itself—and which on state· ment would so engage the consent and affections of the people, as to secure its adoption by Congress.

If this matter be left to politicians, or be hurried through Congress by busy men, it will want all profound merits. It will be sure to violate our American principles, to wound political economy, and to botch the whole idea. If, on the other hand, we can slowly mature a wise, ripe plan, it may become a germ of the utmost beneficence to the soldiers and to the nation.

We are very anxious to have a careful report on the subject of the foreign institutions for the care of invalid soldiers, before the next meeting of Congress. And at the meeting of the Executive Committee of the Sanitary Commission recently held at my house, the following resolution was offered by Mr. Olmsted, and passed:

Resolved, That S. G. Perkins, Esq., be requested to study the military pension and invalid system of the principal European nations, visiting the more important establishments in which invalid soldiers are maintained, and to report his observations to the Commission, with the conclusions of his judgment in regard to an invalid and pension system for the disabled soldiers of the present war.

I hope you will consent to do this work for us. I know no man so well fitted, and I really think it can be laid upon you as a clear call of Divine Providence. Nothing was said on the subject of remuneration. We are all volunteers in this good work. But I think there is no doubt that any necessary expenses, incurred in this service, extra to your natural expenses, would be cheerfully reimbursed by this Commission; and, if this is a point of interest or importance, I will have action taken upon it at the earliest moment.

I have not felt at liberty to withold this communication, although, since the resolution was passed, instructing me to make it, so serious a calamity has fallen upon you. If the sympathy of numerous friends can alleviate your great trial, you will not want much consolation in so profound a sorrow.

I am, dear sir, very respectfully and cordially,

Yours,

HENRY W. BELLOWS,

President of the Sanitary Commission.

REPORT.

Florence, May 22, 1863.

Rev. Henry W. Bellows,
  President of the U. S. Sanitary Commission :

Dear Sir,—In accordance with a resolution passed by your Board, and communicated to me on the 15th of August last, requesting me " to study the military pension and invalid " systems of the principal European nations, visiting the more " important establishments in which invalid soldiers are main- " tained, and to report ' my ' observations to the Commission, " with the conclusions of ' my ' judgment in regard to an in- " valid and pension system for the disabled soldiers of the " present war," I beg leave now to report :

That immediately upon my arrival in France, in September last, I began to make the inquiries indicated, by personal ap- plication in Paris, and by opening a correspondence in the various capitals of Europe. After about seven weeks' delay in Paris, I proceeded to Berlin, whence I intended going to St. Petersburgh, but finding the season too far advanced, I was forced to depend entirely upon correspondence there, and went from Berlin to Vienna, and thence came to Italy. I have already forwarded to you from France and Germany, and from this place, a number of documents, printed and manuscript, containing the various pension laws and tariffs, and a number of details relating to the invalid hospitals, especially of France and Italy, all which, so far as they elucidate the subject, please to consider as attached to this report.

I proposed to myself in beginning the inquiry, to obtain answers as far as possible, to the following queries :

1. The nature of the service, or the injuries which entitle a soldier to receive a pension.

2. The minimum and maximum rates of pension for the common soldiers and principal officers.

3. The rates allowed to widows and orphans.

4. The whole number of military pensions, distinguishing those of officers, soldiers, and widows.

5. The whole amount of pensions paid in 1861, distinguishing the amounts paid to officers, soldiers, and their widows.

6. The nature of service or injury giving a right to enter invalid hospitals or societies.

7. The terms on which such entry is accorded, especially as relating to the continued receipt or the abandonment of the pensions.

8. The number of invalid hospitals, and of their inmates, their situation, &c.

9. Total cost of maintaining the hospitals, including everything excepting rent.

10. The occupation of the inmates, and such further details as might seem useful.

11. What other provision (out of hospital and besides pension) is made for invalids.

The annexed table shows, briefly stated, the answers to these queries, as far as I have obtained them, and so arranged that a comparison can be made between the different nations enumerated. It will be seen that in France and Italy, the provision for the common soldier, as well in regard to the terms on which the pension and the right of admission to hospital are accorded, as to rates of pension allowed, and to the care of their widows and children, is far more just and humane than that existing in Germany. Indeed, in Prussia and Austria, the minimum pension of the common soldier is a mere pittance, which can go but very little way towards supporting him, and only those most severely injured gain admission to the hospitals. In France, the pensions have been raised several times, and the minimum now for the common soldier, is one franc a day. In Italy, it is about fifty-five centimes; in Prussia, twelve thalers *a year;* and in Austria, five kreutzers (say two cents) a day.

The average of all the pensions of subalterns and soldiers in Austria, appears to be only twenty-eight florins per annum, or say between three and four cents a day.

Another striking contrast is shown by the table, in the treatment of officers and soldiers. In France, about one-fifth of the pensions is paid to officers, and the amount so paid is about fifteen thirty-thirds of the whole payment, whereas in Prussia, only one-sixth of the pensions belongs to officers, but it absorbs twenty-eight thirty-thirds of the payment, while in Austria, the pensions of the officers and their widows are one-fourth of the whole number, and absorb about twenty-eight thirty-thirds of the whole payment. In contrasting France and Italy, we find that although the rates of pensions are about the same (allowing for the cost of living), and the terms of admission both into the ranks of the pensioners and into the invalid establishments are very similar, the practice of the pensioners is quite different. While in France, the number in hospital is constantly diminishing, and the inmates and admissions consist almost entirely of men over sixty years of age, and the whole number of invalids is only about two thousand, with a pension list of over fifty-seven thousand, in Italy there are over ten thousand men in the hospitals, with a pension list of about thirty thousand. It is true, that a certain number of these are men left in hospital by the government lately expelled from Naples, but the contrast is highly honorable to the French character. The returns from all these countries agree in one particular, and a very important one for our consideration, viz., that, in consequence of the laws establishing pensions and hospitals having been made at different times, and without due regard to each other, there is no just proportion between the cost of maintenance of the invalids in hospital and the rates of pension allowed, even where the latter are the most liberal. Either the former is too high, or the latter is too low. Probably, the cost in hospital is everywhere much too high.

Dr. Faure, Medical Director of the Invalides, states that in the year 1861 there was an average number of 2,302 invalids in the Hotel des Invalides in Paris, and that the cost of maintaining them, including all salaries, and the charges for repairs of the Hotel, but no rent, was frs. 2,313,744.41, equal to frs. 1,005.10 per head.

On the 25th of October, 1862, there remained in the establishment 2,099 invalids, viz. :

1 chef de bataillon,	58 caporaux sous-officiers,
15 capitaines,	33 sergent-majors,
23 lieutenants,	354 sergents,
23 sous-lieutenants,	281 caporaux,
33 chefs et adjts. de division,	1,250 soldats,
12 adjts. sous-officiers,	16 tambours.
107	1,992
	107
	2,099 invalids.

The amount of pensions which would have been paid to these persons, had they not entered the hospital, would have been, as nearly as can be ascertained, frs. 1,150,890, or, say, frs. 548.30 average, per man. They cost the State, therefore, nearly twice as much in hospital, as the amount of their pensions. One reason of this is, that the Hotel is fitted to accommodate about double the present number of inmates, but there is, also, a great deal of useless expense.

A similar result is found in Italy, where the hospitals are crowded. I have not at hand the data for calculating the pensions to which the invalids would be entitled, but the general figures show the result. Thus, 10,759 persons in hospital cost frs. 6,388,593 per annum, while the amount of 30,229 pensions, including officers, is only frs. 15,748,328. The contrast is still greater in Germany. The 480 invalids in hospital in Prussia cost more in proportion to the average of pension than the French invalids do ; and in Austria, where the average of all the pensions of subalterns and soldiers is only florins 28 per annum, the average cost of 200 officers, and 201 soldiers and subalterns, in the six hospitals and Filialien, is florins 162 per head per annum. The general conclusion is, that all laws establishing pensions and invalid hospitals should be made with reference to each other.

Although there may be no features in the European systems above referred to, which are to be recommended as models to be copied, still I think we may gain from the examination of them, not only knowledge of what we ought to avoid, but also some ideas which we may apply in framing our law. The great point to be avoided, and yet one which seems to have been almost everywhere overlooked, is the failure to provide regular civil occupation for the invalids. For want of this, it has been found impossible at the Hotel des Invalides, in Paris, to prevent drunkenness. Dr. Faure, the head physician of that establishment, told me that it was common for the invalids to sell their rations of meat and bread, in order to obtain the means to buy brandy, and that nearly all the punishments which they were forced to inflict, arose from drunkenness. Other officers of that establishment corroborated his statement, and all said, if you establish an invalid hospital system, let regular occupation for invalids be the corner-stone of it.

As regards the features which may be imitated with adaptations to our peculiar condition, there are, perhaps, two. First, the Prussian civil-versorgung-scheins, of which there is a particular account in the documents I sent you from Berlin ; and, secondly, the Prussian and Italian plan of dividing all the invalids into two classes—one still fit for stationary military duty, and one unfit for any military duty, from the former of which the garrisons, in certain proportions, are recruited. By extending this to all pensions, and allowing those fitted for service to volunteer for garrison duty, perhaps a considerable number of pensioners might be saved, as it is presumable that the United States Government will be obliged to maintain numerous garrisons for many years after the present war shall have come to an end. Probably, likewise, a number of men might volunteer, especially among our naturalized citizens, for the sake of exchanging their pensions for the full pay of a soldier, and with light duties in garrison service.

As regards the civil-versorgung-scheins, they may be described as warrants issued to military pensioners 'by government, securing them appointments to the first places vacant in certain subordinate branches of *civil* service (such as the railroads, post-offices, custom-houses, &c.), for which they may be found fit, to the exclusion of competitors from civil life. There are said to be about fifteen hundred of these issued annually, and and as fast as they are provided with places in the civil service, they are stricken off the pension list. This system is very economical for the government, but in Prussia it works a great evil, by building up a military caste among the lower orders of society, analogous to the one which exists among the upper classes. In the United States, I think we should have little to fear on this score, and as our Government is obliged to maintain a multitude of subordinate officers in the custom-houses, the post-offices, &c., it might be no disadvantage to have half the number consist of men entitled to hold their places during good behavior, and so removed from the corrupting influences of political changes. The war must leave us a very large number of young invalids to provide for, and it is very important, therefore, for economical and other reasons, that a variety of occupations should be offered to them, so that the different tastes and habits of the men may be suited, as far as possible, and the number of idle pensioners in the republic reduced to the utmost; and no invalid ought to be left in the position to complain, that with a pension less than sufficient to support him, he is forced to compete in the open labor market with able-bodied men.

In the following schedule of a pension and hospital law, which I have concluded to submit to the consideration of the Board, I have endeavored to combine this variety with such features as appear to me to be important :

Proposed Schedule of Pension and Hospital Laws.

1. That every officer and soldier permanently disabled by wounds or sickness during the present war, shall be entitled to a pension from the United States Government.

2. That there shall be three rates of pensions, viz : A *maximum* rate, sufficient to support the pensioner according to his rank, with due economy, to be accorded to those who have suffered injuries *equal* to the loss of two limbs; a *medium* rate, to be accorded to those who have received injuries equal to the loss of one limb ; and a *minimum* rate for all minor injuries.

2

3. That the widows and orphans of those who have died from wounds, or disease, *be allowed one-half the maximum rate*, payable to the widows during life, if they remain unmarried; to the boys, until they reach 21 years of age; and to the girls, until that age, or their previous marriage.

4. That all the pensioners be divided into two classes—one, fit for garrison, or other stationary military service, and one, unfit for such service, and that the garrisons be recruited to the extent of one-half their number, from volunteers of the former class, who shall receive full pay and rations, but abandon their pensions while in service. On being honorably discharged, they shall have the right to resume their pensions.

5. That all pensioners shall have the right to be appointed to certain subordinate employments in the civil service of the United States, within the States to which they respectively belong (Custom-Houses, Post-Offices, &c.) in preference to other competitors, on making proper application, and showing fitness for the office asked for. That such persons, on getting their appointment, shall abandon their pensions, *without* any right to resume them, but be entitled to hold their appointments during good behavior.

6. That the U. S. Government shall establish in every State, in some central and healthy situation, an invalid industrial village, to consist of buildings intended as boarding-houses for unmarried men, to contain not over one hundred boarders in any one house, and of small cottages, to be let to married invalids, or such as prefer to keep house for themselves.

7. That these establishments shall be under strict military government, and each be the residence of a pension agent for

the State in which it is situated, acting under the central agency in Washington.

That occupations of various kinds, agricultural and manufacturing, and suited, as far as possible, to the capabilities of men disabled in various ways, be established in these villages, and all invalids able to work, who may inhabit them, be obliged to work, and be *paid wages according to the value of their labor.* Said wages to be fixed by an officer or board appointed for the purpose.

8. That all pensioners shall have the right of admission into these hospitals (each within his own State), with an option between two arrangements, viz. : either (a) to retain his pension and pay all his own expenses, including board if he live in a large house, or house-hire and his own provisions, if he prefer to keep house, or, (b) to abandon his pension and be fed and lodged by Government, merely clothing himself from his wages ; with the right, however, to resume his pension and pay his own expenses after he has attained skill in the new work he may have to learn—say after one year's apprenticeship.

9. That any pensioner in hospital shall have the right to leave the hospital and resume his pension, if he had abandoned it, after one year's stay, and by giving three months' notice, but that in this case he shall not be entitled to return to it.

10. That the products shall belong to the United States, and be applied, as far as possible, to the use of the invalid establishments.

I remain, dear Sir,

Very respectfully,

Your obt. Servt.,

STEPHEN H. PERKINS.

A COMPARATIVE VIEW OF THE PENSION AND INVALID SYSTEMS IN DIFFERENT COUNTRIES.

	FRANCE.	PRUSSIA.	AUSTRIA.	ITALY.	RUSSIA.	REMARKS.
The nature of the Service or Injuries which entitle a Soldier to a Pension	Length of service, and Injuries and diseases of a permanent kind.	Same as France.	Injuries precluding the possibility of further military service.	Same as France.		The details as to time of service, character of injuries, &c., differ in every country. See detailed laws.
The maximum and minimum rates of Pensions for the Common Soldier	FOR OFFICERS. ... 465 258	FOR ARMEN. Thalers. ... 84 18	FOR MEN. Kreutzers. ... 70 5	FOR ARMEN. France ... 156 900		For officers' pensions, see detailed tables.
Provision of Widows and Orphans	One quarter of the maximum, when the soldier dies from injuries.	Nothing to widows of common soldiers.	Nothing to widows of common soldiers.	One-half maximum when pensioner dies from wounds. One-quarter of pension if from other cause.		Unusual attempts have been made to increase the officers' widows' pensions in France.
Whole number of Invalid Pensions	PENSIONS OF Officers ... 18,166 Soldiers and Subalterns ... 14,402 ——— 32,566	PENSIONS OF Officers ... 1,965 Soldiers and Subalterns ... 21,435 ——— 23,400	PENSIONS OF OFFICERS, &c. Non-combatants ... 11,165 Officers' Widows ... 6,453 Soldiers and Subalterns ... 82,604 ——— 99,450	All military pensions, 96,300.		The number in France varies largely, where so many go into civil life.
Amount of Pensions paid per Annum	1841. OFFICERS' PENSIONS. France ... 14,642,648 Soldiers and Subalterns ... 10,651,265 ——— France ... 25,293,913	1841. SUBALTERNS' PENSIONS. Thalers ... 2,789,611 Soldiers and Subalterns ... 570,128 ——— Thalers ... 8,358,789	1841. Florins. Officers, &c. ... 7,945,162 Widows of ... 305,614 ——— 8,748,909 Soldiers and Subalterns ... 1,863,008 ——— Florins ... 10,595,062	1841. TOTAL OF MILITARY PENSIONS. Amount, France ... 15,340,345		The proportion paid to officers in Germany is excessive.
The nature of Service, or of Injury, giving a right to enter Invalid Establishments	Sixty years of age and the receipt of pension, or injuries equal to the loss of one limb.	The severest kinds of injury, blindness, and insanity.	Same as in Prussia.	All injuries of a permanent kind, and old age.		In Germany, only a portion of totally disabled can find room in hospital.
Terms of Entry, to regulate Relinquishment of Pensions	Pensions cease on entering but may be reclaimed on leaving Hospital.	Pensions cease.	Pensions continue, and the invalids are supported beside.	Special provision in the way of pay is made, and invalids pay their own expenses.		The forms in Austria are very liable to the severely wounded. Detailed report for the Italian particulars.
Number of the Invalid Establishments and of Invalids	One Hospital in Paris. 2,712 Invalids.	Two hospitals, 460 inmates; seven invalid companies, 651 members.	Three hospitals, three "Filiation," 2,001 Invalids.	Two hospitals; 10,675 invalids.		Another large hospital is to be erected in Florence; to refer to the one in Paris.
Total Annual Cost of Maintenance, exclusive of Rent	1841. Frs. 2,313,764 41.		1881. Florins, 199,215.	1841. Frs. 8,565,692.		Including cost of the schools &c.
Occupation of Invalids	Some small offices in the Hotel.	"Half Invalids" are drafted for garrison duty. No employment in the Hospital.	None.	Able bodied men drafted into garrisons, &c. Music and Grammar schools.		See detailed reports from France, Italy.
Other provision for Invalids out of Hospital and beside Pension	None.	The seven invalid companies above named, are quartered in the hospital itself, in different parts of the kingdom, at government expense. The civil vermessungsbehörde system.	Three "Filiation," similar to the Prussian invalid companies.	None.		Details of the Prussian civil establishment system given in report from Berlin.

APPENDIX.

FRANCE.

Summary of the Pension and Hospital System of France for the Relief of Permanent Military Invalids.

1st. *Pensions.*—The laws relating to military pensions, are numerous and detailed.

2d. The progress has been towards raising the rates of the various tariffs, applicable to pensioners for long service, for wounds, widows, &c.

3d. The last law (of June, 1861) fixes the pension of the common soldier, at *minimum rate* .... frs. 365
Maximum, (excepting under an extraordinary combination of claims,) 465
And, under certain possible circumstances, rarely occurring, it can reach .... : 725
(all per annum.)
A General of Divisions has—*minimum* 5,200
" " " " *maximum* 7,800
Possible under certain combinations 11,232

There is a great variety of rates for officers of inferior rank. A Marshal of France *may* receive as much as frs. 20,000 pension at the pleasure of the Emperor.

4th. Widows and orphans receive one quarter of the maximum.

5th. The number of new pensions granted in 1860, was, for long service 1,778
For injuries....................................... 1,702
Under the "Réforme" law 19
To widows and orphans........................ 614
                                                      ———
                                                      4,113

6th. The whole number of pensions granted from 1 January, 1855, to 1 October, 1862, was :

Long service.....................................	
For injuries.....................................	8,669
To widows and orphans..........................	6,174

Making for seven years and nine months......... 14,843
pensions arising from loss by war.

7th. The whole number of military pensioners on the 1st January, 1861, was............................ 57,366
Of these 10,764 received officers' pensions.
       46,602   "   soldiers' or subalterns'.

57,366

8th. The whole amount of military pensions 1st January, 1861, was............................... frs. 33,395,911
Of which belonged to officers............. " 14,863,646
  "   "   " soldiers and subalterns " 18,532,265

frs. 33,395,911

9th. Whole amount of the new pensions granted
   the year 1860........................ frs. 2,200,000
Average for 5 *years*, to 1st January, 1861, per
   annum................................. " 2,639,999
Average for 30 years to do. do............. " 1,975,265

Remarks.

1st. It appears from the above that the average rate of all persons, is about frs. 550 per annum, including officers, soldiers, and widows.

2d. The sum of frs. 33,000,000 does not include naval pensions, nor civil pensions. The latter, I suppose, amount to a large sum.

3d. The *number* of military pensions has rapidly decreased, as the men of the first Empire have died off. In 1821 there were 122,141 pensioners receiving frs. 46,784,628, as stated by Cardinal Mathieu, who has made a study of the subject.

4th. The widow's pension of $\frac{1}{4}$ the maximum, seems *too small*. It is true that going to the orphan it is slowly extinguished. Cardinal Mathieu calculates that it requires over 60 years to extinguish such a list.

Invalid Hospitals.

1st. The French Government have been gradually diminishing the number of Hospitals. There were formerly several in the Provinces, now there remains only the Hotel des Invalides in Paris.

2d. The number of inmates in this hospital is gradually piminishing. The deaths exceed in number the admissions In 1854, there were 3,027 inmates; in October, 1862, only 2,099.

3d. The admissions consist of soldiers in receipt of a pension, who have *either* attained the age of sixty years, or sustained an injury *equal* to the loss of one limb.

4th. On entering the hospital, the invalid must resign his pension; but he can leave the hospital, and resume it again, if he choose. In such case, he cannot return.

5th. The admissions consist chiefly of men over 60 years of age, and the average age of the inmates is now about 70 years. Since the year 1855, only 283 men under 51 years of age have entered, and only 527 men under 61 years of age.

6th. The cost, in 1861, of feeding, clothing, and governing an average of 2,302 invalids, including all salaries and wages, and the *cost of repairs* of the Hotel (exclusive of rent), was frs. 2,313,744.41, *equal to frs.* 2.75 *per head per diem!*

7th. The amount of *pensions surrendered* by these invalids is about frs. 1,150,890—equal *to frs.* 1.50 *per head per day!*

8th. Government provides no employment for the invalids. They are allowed to find work for themselves in the city, and some do so ; a considerable number are, however, idlers and drunkards.

Remarks.

1st. The number of invalids in hospital will probably diminish for some years to come, as the young men who are entitled to enter generally prefer to remain at home; and the increase of frs. 165 per annum, made in 1861, to the soldiers' pension, will tend to confirm this habit. Therefore, the cost per head of maintaining the inmates will increase. As shown above, it now exceeds the pensions to the amount of over a franc a head a day. This shows the importance of having the pension and hospital laws and arrangements such as *not to throw a loss upon the government by giving an option to the pensioner.*

2d. The fact that so few young men enter is highly creditable to the French character, and shows, I think, that with a rate of pensions considerably short of the cost of living, few young men, with us, would go to the hospital with a prospect of a bare maintenance.

3d. It is, therefore, desirable to leave them their pensions, and their own charges, and find them work, giving them certain options, which shall leave the cost to the State as nearly as possible the same, whichever choice the invalid may make.

Comparison of the MAXIMUM *Pensions, (where two limbs are lost after 12 years active service,) and the present cost of keeping the same men and officers at the "Invalides."*

	At the Invalides, October, 1862.		Maximum Pension.			Total Cost.
1	Chief of Battalion, (Major)	Frs.	3,730	each.	Frs.	3,730
15	Captains,	"	3,053	"	"	45,795
23	Lieutenants,	"	2,419	"	"	55,637
23	Second Lieutenants,	"	2,016	"	"	46,368
33	Chiefs and Adjutants of Division	"	2,000	"	"	66,000
58	Corporals, (acting lieutenants)	"	788	"	"	45,704
12	Adjutants, second officers,	"	1,193	"	"	14,316
33	Sergeant Majors,	"	1,037	"	"	34,221
354	Sergeants,	"	881	"	"	311,874
281	Corporals,	"	788	"	"	221,428
1,250	Soldiers,	"	725	"	"	906,250
16	Drummers,	"	725	"	"	11,600
2,099	Number of Men and officers.		{ Cost in francs of highest pensions }			1,762,923

This gives, say, frs. 840 per head per annum or *frs.* 2.30 *per head per day.*

N. B. — Dr. FAURE's statement shows a total expense for 1861, including *repairs* of the Hotel des Invalides of frs. 2,313,744.41.

If you divide this sum by 2,302 (the *average number* in the hotel in 1861), you have : Frs. 1,005.10, as the cost per head per annum = to, say, frs. 2.75 *per head per diem,* deducting cost of repairs.

It gives frs. 951 per an. = frs. 2.60 per head per diem.

The expense in hospital is, therefore, from 30 to 45 centimes more than the *maximum* pensions, and seems to be quite high. This shows the disadvantage of a *large establishment,* not capable of being suited to changing numbers. As the number of invalids has diminished, the cost per head has been increasing.

The real difference between the pensions and the cost in hospital is more likely to be 75 centimes, or over, than less ; because only a limited number of the inmates would draw a *maximum* pension if they remained outside.

The present rate of pensions (being for a General of Division from frs. 5,200 to 11,200, according to circumstances, and for a soldier from frs. 365 to 725), induces nearly all the younger invalids to live at home, and get what work they can. The admissions to the "Invalides" since the war of the Crimea have consisted *mostly of men of* 60 *years of age and over*—a considerable number over 80 years old, and some over 90, have come in. The qualification for admission is an injury equal to the loss of one limb, or 25 years of active service ; in fact, the prerequisite condition, in all cases, is the enjoyment of a pension, which pension the applicant must *resign if he enter hospital.* If he leave the hospital he can claim his pension again, but he cannot return to the hospital. Most of the present admissions consist of old soldiers, who have got along on the old (lower) rate of pensions until their strength or their friends failed, and then came in, one after the other, never to go out again alive. Under these circumstances the numbers in hospital necessarily diminish, and must continue to do so rapidly for some years. In 1851, there were 3,165 inmates, and in 1861, 2,430 only. The deaths exceed the admissions, and as there may not be any increase in the number of the admissions until the invalids of the late wars grow old, Dr. Faure thinks the number may diminish to 1,000, perhaps, which may cause some change in the establishment. In 1851, at the time M. Bilco undertook the administration, it was first put under the control of the Minister of War, and an economical reform took place ; but it is still fitted to lodge 4,000 invalids. Before 1851 it had an independent government, as originally planned by Louis XIV. The great difficulty at the "Invalides" is, that there is no regular employment for the men. They are allowed to find work and wages for themselves, out of the house if they can, merely answering at morning and evening roll-call, and they can even get permission to remain out by showing good cause; some do this, but most of them, though able to work, either cannot find it or prefer idleness. They sell their allowance of bread (three loaves a day), and even of meat sometimes, and become loungers and drunkards, to a considerable extent. All the officers whom I have seen have said to me, at once, " If you have invalid hospitals, give the men employment." This must be the fundamental principle. Although the young French invalids show a very creditable spirit of independence in getting along on their

TARIFF OF PENSIONS FOR OFFICERS AND EMPLOYES OF ASSIMILATED RANK, IN THE FRENCH ARMY.

	Existing Pension for length of service. (Art. 9th, Act of April 11th, 1831.)			RETIRING PENSIONS On account of Wounds, or serious or incurable Infirmities. (Articles 12, 13, 14, 15, 16, 17 of the Act of April 11, 1831.)					

Fr. | Fr. | Fr. | Fr. | Fr. | Fr. | Fr. | Fr. | Fr. | Fr. | Fr.

pensions, as well as they can, and the numbers in hospital are diminishing, I think it would be a mistake to suppose that the "Invalides" can be ever dispensed with. There is always a certain number quite unable to get on elsewhere—men badly injured and without friends to help them. Then, again, those who undertake to keep themselves know that when friends and wages fail they can always resort, at last, to the "Invalides;" and they exert themselves more cheerfully, and come into hospital gradually, as they grow old or weak. With us there are several important reasons, not existing here, for the establish ment of invalid hospitals, where work can be always found and fairly remunerated ; but even here a hospital of some kind will be always needed, and one without work is better than none.

PENSIONS ANNUALLY GRANTED, UNDER THE ACT OF APRIL 11, 1831.

| | RETIRING PENSIONS. | | | | WIDOWS' PENSIONS AND ANNUAL RELIEF FOR ORPHANS. | |
| | For Length of Service. | | For Wounds and Infirmities. | | | |
	Number.	Amount.	Number.	Amount.	Number.	Amount.
1831	1,290	1,397,679	32	19,725	783	276,825
1832	1,241	1,715,139	531	299,016	1,165	422,225
1833	1,895	2,148,024	361	136,594	1,165	316,850
1834	3,014	2,837,182	300	110,900	909	274,450
1835	2,195	2,318,605	238	77,418	769	227,050
1836	1,532	1,734,768	113	47,417	826	223,900
1837	1,561	1,734,830	154	58,967	604	165,775
1838	1,303	1,448,470	194	77,632	582	166,365
1839	1,543	1,679,681	177	69,449	760	235,225
1840	1,403	1,387,258	196	78,431	845	216,875
1841	1,192	1,211,615	318	100,989	846	252,650
1842	809	788,415	270	190,681	558	168,775
1843	1,201	1,205,731	293	93,459	743	206,800
1844	1,310	1,215,893	290	102,622	665	192,375
1845	1,364	1,364,005	234	78,952	772	232,900
1846	1,458	1,259,617	234	83,458	604	176,775
1847	1,367	1,193,383	301	113,636	694	201,275
1848	1,689	2,708,663	247	86,046	770	239,825
1849	1,516	1,221,788	265	90,503	691	208,400
1850	1,261	1,237,957	329	. 101,694	610	185,600
1851	1,411	1,186,640	296	101,082	837	235,750
1852	1,978	1,700,954	288	108,619	915	289,950
1853	1,518	1,230,362	314	123,958	578	170,650
1854	1,849	1,540,129	264	163,919	918	267,850
1855	1,126	1,178,255	570	273,791	733	256,581
1856	1,587	1,412,778	3,069	1,365,227	965	341,910
1857	3,619	2,413,493	1,380	606,175	794	210,633
1858	2,991	2,123,891	597	289,428	800	227,189
1859	2,272	1,702,251	378	192,584	732	219,933
1860	1,778	1,250,245	1,699	757,119	614	192,579
Total	50,283	47,384,901	13,931	5,849,313	22,229	7,063,450
Average for each of the 30 years,	1,761	1,579,392	464	193,643	741	235,448

EXTRACT FROM *Moniteur* OF 25TH JUNE, 1861.

Whole amount of Pensions 1st Jan'y, 1861................frs. 33,395,911
" number of pensioners............................ 57,366
Of these officers......... ..... 10,764, receiving pensions......frs. 14,863,646
" soldiers and subalterns, 46,602, " " ......" 18,532,265
Average of pensions, 1860.................................." 539
" amount of pensions granted for five years, per annum..." 2,639,999

The first remark I make in reviewing the French laws and establishment, is the necessity of having the Pension and Invalid Hospital laws arranged in their details with reference to each other.

Secondly, The importance of fixing such a scale of pensions that the pensioners cannot live on them in idleness unless assisted by friends.

Thirdly, The advantage of giving invalids *a choice*, under certain restrictions, between pension and hospital assistance ; and,

Fourthly, The importance of having the pension laws and regulations as simple as possible, consistently with exactness. With us invalid hospitals for the mere purpose of finding work, and taking the men out of the streets and bar-rooms, will be needed. Let all those who can support themselves by labor at home do so—the sooner the better—but let no man be supported in idleness outside, and none inside the hospital who can work; and further, let no man be able to say, "I cannot live on my pension, and I cannot find work."

PRUSSIA.

The result of the inquiry here is that Prussia has a voluminous and complicated system of pensions, but they are made almost entirely in the interest of the officer or noble class. The common soldier is turned aside with a very small pittance, or provided for by putting him into civil service, to the exclusion of civilians, by means of the system of "Versorgungs-Scheins." The case contrasts very poorly with that of France.

Invalids are disposed of in five ways—

1st. They receive their pension and live at home.

2d. " go into invalid hospitals.

3d. " join invalid companies.

4th. " are drafted into the reserve battalion.

5th. " receive civil-versorgungs-scheins—that is, papers authorizing them to claim vacant places, within their ability, in post-offices, railroads, and other Government employments. Of these some 1,500 are stated to be issued annually, and as fast as the holders find places equal to their pensions, they are struck off the list of pensioners, and so relieve Government, at the expense of other candidates for the places. This must reduce the list fast, and yet it seems quite large in proportion to the army and the circumstances of the country.

The whole number of pensioners is 25,000 ; of these, 4,000 officers.

Whole amount spent yearly on pensions, thalers 3,358,736, of which officers receive......   thalers 2,788,611
" "   soldiers "   "   570,125

A very striking contrast with France, where the officers constitute one-fifth of the pensioners, and receive only $\frac{11}{33}$ds of the fund.

The soldiers' pension here is indeed nominal, viz., *minimum* per annum................................... 12 thalers.
Mamimum (when blind or without arms)........ 84 "
A thaler being, say 72 cents, in ordinary times. As Mr. Fay explains the complications of the system, I will refer to his letter for particulars.

The invalid hospitals are but two, and contain only 480 inmates. Their cost is even greater here than in Paris, in proportion to the rate of pensions and of living.

The invalid companies appear to be intended to take the place of hospitals. There are seven of them distributed about the kingdom, containing 651 members who have resigned their pensions, and are quartered on the inhabitants; of these, 51 are officers.

The reserved battalion consists of such men as are but little injured, and are drafted for garrison service, and receive wages. They come from the class of "half invalids."

N. B.—Perhaps we might do something in this way; of course, leaving it voluntary. For we shall have need of large garrisons for many years.

The civil-versorgungs-scheins constitute the peculiar feature, however, of the Prussian system. They tend here to establish a permanent military caste among the lower orders, just as already exists among the upper, and are, I suppose, favored by the latter for that reason.

The effect must, however, be very unfavorable for the numerous poor applicants for places in the subordinate branches of the civil service.

Extract from Letter of Hon. THEODORE S. FAY.

*   *   *   *   *   *   *   *

And first the system of military pensions:

Prussia maintains at this moment 200,000 effective men, at the cost of 40 million thalers.

Until 1825, no law existed respecting pensions to officers.
3

Pensions were granted as a matter of favor. Even after the wars of Napoleon the expenditure amounted only to half a million for officers and soldiers. No officer received any pension without first giving his word that he had no other sufficient means of livelihood.

On the 4th June, 1851, the law, at present in force, regulating pensions of common soldiers and under officers, was published by the late king, with the consent of the Chambers. It is entitled, "Law concerning the support of military invalids from the Oberfeuerwerker (chief gunner), Feldwebel (sergeant), and Wachtmeister (sergeant in the cavalry) down." (Thus, not including superior officers.) It comprehends persons who have become invalid in active service or in consequence of it. The same principle applies to all without distinction of kind of weapons or of troops. The pensioners are divided into half invalid and wholly invalid. By half invalid is understood those entirely disabled for military service in the field, although not for home military duty in garrison, towns, fortresses, &c. The wholly invalid are disabled absolutely for every kind of military duty, both in the field and at home.

They are subdivided into four classes :

1. Those entirely disabled for every kind of work.
2. Those for the most part disabled.
3. Those partly disabled.
4. Those slightly disabled, but always in such a way as to wholly disqualify him for military service. A man may be in perfect health, and able to perform work of various kinds, and yet wholly disqualified for military service, by the loss of his little finger.

Pensions are divided into four classes, and persons entitled to pensions are divided into four grades.

REMARK.—I have, for the sake of clearness, used the word *grade* to designate the four classes of persons entitled to pensions, and the word *class* to designate the four different amounts of pensions. The law uses the word *class* for both.

The amount of the pensions is monthly :

	1. Class.		2. Class.		3. Class.		4. Class.	
	Thlrs.	Sqr.	Thlrs.	Sqr.	Thlrs.	Sqr.	Thlrs.	Sqr.
Grade 1. For Oberfeuerwerker Feldwebel & Wachtmeister...	8		6		5		3	
Grade 2. For Vicefeldwebel & Sergeanten	6		5		4		2	15
Grade 3. For Teuerwerker and Unterofficiere	5		4		3		2	
Grade 4. For the other soldiers.	3	15	2	25	2		1	

Each of these four grades, as is seen, thus receives a different pension according as he is—

1. Entirely disabled for every kind of work.
2. For the most part disabled for every kind of work.
3. Partly disabled for every kind of work.
4. Slightly disabled for every kind of work, but always in such a way as to wholly disqualify him for military service.

Pensions are given, however, not only to persons who have been wounded, or become invalid in, or in consequence of, military duty, but to such as have become weakened and disqualified by the mere length of their service, without any absolute malady.

A. HALF INVALID.

The half invalid has a right to a pension after—

a. A service of twelve years, or
b. A possessor of a military order won in war, or
c. Wounded on the battle-field, or
d. Injury received in actual service, or
e. Attack of a contagious eye malady during active military service.

These have the choice either to receive a wholly invalid pension of the fourth grade, or to be placed, according to their rank, in a garrison, or fortress, &c.

The term "contagious eye malady" requires an explanation. The French soldiers brought back from Egypt a strange affection, the eyelids becoming inflamed and turning inside out. The inflammation is increased by dusty marches, and loss of sight often followed. The Prussian authorities declare it contagious. It is probably unknown among us.

B. Wholly Invalid.

The wholly invalid has a right to the first-class pension.

a. After having served at least 21 years, or

b. Who have in time of war won a Prussian military order, or

c. Who have been wounded on the battle-field, or

d. Who have been injured in direct military service (excluding all but direct service), or

e. Who have become entirely blind from contagious malady in the eyes, during active military service.

Second-class pensions are given to wholly invalid persons in a great degree unable to support themselves, after 15 years' service, on the same conditions as preceding section.

Third-class pensions are given to the wholly invalid—

a. After 12 years' service, or

b. Possessing an order as before, or

c. Who have become partly unable to support themselves, in consequence of certain causes designated in section 10 of the law.

Fourth-class pensions as designated section II.

Mutilated, or quite blind, invalids are in every case counted as entirely unable to support themselves.

Invalids receiving first-class pensions when mutilated or quite blind, without distinction of grade, receive an additional pension in the following cases and decrees :

Loss of two arms, thlr. 3.15 sgr. monthly.

" " the right arm, thlrs. 2. — "

" " the left arm, " 1. 15 sgr. "

" " two feet, " 1. — "

Complete blindness of both eyes, thlrs. 2.15 sgur. monthly.

The 14th section of the law supposes the case of a person who may claim one of the higher classes of pension by this length of service, but who, notwithstanding, is not really disabled from gaining his support, a lower pension will be accorded to such a person according to the actual degree of his disablement. For instance, the loss of a finger classes a man with the wholly invalid, and after a service of 21 years entitles him to the invalid pension of the first class ; but if, in other respects, his health is

good enough to permit him to work at his profession, a lower
pension is substituted.

Oberfeuerwerker ( ), Feldwebel, ( ),
Wachtmeister, ( ), entitled to pensions of the first
class receive instead of the same, higher pensions, after

30 years' service, 10 thlrs. monthly.

40 " " 12 " "

50 " " 15 " "

In the invalid houses,* and invalid companies,† the wholly
invalid, who have claim to the first-class pensions, are received
by preference before the others; the mutilated by the loss of an
arm or a foot, before such as are not mutilated; and, of course,
those having lost two arms or two feet, or the entirely blind,
before the rest. Of those accepted, only a fourth part must be
married persons, and must not bring with them children over
fourteen years.

The claim of a soldier must be properly presented for examination before released from the service.

Soldiers becoming invalid after quitting the service receive
pensions of the fourth class, when they have won an order in
war as above, or when their invalid state results from the causes
stipulated in the other sections.

Persons not military, but in military service, have, under certain modifications and regulations, the same claim to pensions
as military persons; for instance, arsenal gunsmiths, &c.

I have given above a resumé of the pension law of 1851, for
common soldiers. The principle upon which it is founded,
perhaps cannot be understood, except by one acquainted with
the country itself. When I asked what regulated the amount
of the pension, the reply was: "The knowledge of the means

* There are *two* invalid houses in Prussia—one in Berlin with 400 inmates, and
one in Stolpe with 80. Most injuries entitle invalids to admission, but on entering
they relinquish their pensions, which, however, on again coming out they resume.
In these houses they are supplied with everything gratuitously, but *board* and
drink. For this they pay out of their pension 1¼ *groschen* per day.

† Invalid companies are designed to take the place of the hospitals. There are
seven of them, containing 51 officers and 600 men. On entering them the invalid
loses his pension, and is quartered on private families.

of subsistence." It aims at supplying the disabled soldier, who has conducted himself well, and, at the same time, performed his military service, with his daily bread. The pensioner wholly disabled from gaining his own livelihood, can live easily and comfortably upon the sum allotted to him. Take, for example, a common soldier, disabled by the loss of two arms, thus totally unable even to turn a hand organ ; he receives 3 thlrs. 15 sgr. pension, and 3 thl. 15 sgr. additional for tho loss of his arms, in all 88 thlrs. per annum, which may be applied as follows : A comfortable room for 10 thlrs., if unfurnished, a a high estimate, leaving 74 thlrs. for clothing, food and fuel, &c. I am assured, that all the necessaries of life thus lie within reach of this sum, of course, not in cities, and, taking for granted the absence of bad habits, and of every kind of super-fluity, except a little tobacco, and an occasional glass of beer.

To your question, as to what system of employment is estab-lished for the purpose of relieving the government from the support of persons able to support themselves, I answer : Prussia has such a system in her criminal prisons, but not in her military hospitals, as the soldier would consider himself lowered by being put to this kind of forced labor. But the government accomplishes the same purpose in another way. Those who are able to labor receive, what is called, "civil-versor-gungs schein." This is a certificate which entitles the possessor to claim any vacant place in the public service for which he is qualified. The government is thus not only relieved from the charge of the principal part of disabled pensioners, able to work, but secures the services of a large number of tried servants, accustomed to obedience, and bound to it by ties of interest and gratitude. About 1,500 of these certificates are given annually, although the places are not always immediately obtainable. Half invalid persons may choose between three advantages :

1. Pension of the fourth class.
2. Place in a garrison or fortress.
3. Civil-versorgungs schein.

REMARK.—This certificate is never given to an epileptic, nor to any one who has not been distinguished by a good conduct. The old or invalid soldier is thus preferred for every possible place. He is the porter of the public department and offices, the keeper or overseer of the royal palaces and gardens, the conductor and the watchman of the railroad, such as are government property, and with such as are not, it is stipulated on granting the concession that they receive this kind of employé. They compose the numerous personnel of the post-office. They are the letter-carriers and the postillions, and places are found for them in the administration of theatres, operas, &c. The gendarme, the custom-house officer, the constable, the police officer, all these are relieving the government of the weight of the pension system. Even the aged pauper, who receives permission to turn the hand-organ in public promenades, is an old soldier, who pays for his license. I presume, it may be taken for granted, that no pensioner able to work is long without an employment by which the government is relieved.

It is, however, of course, obvious that this great advantage to the military class is at the expense of the civil population, and that many deserving persons, not in the army or in the civil employment of the government find the uniform often before them in the principal paths of preferment, and are thus placed on the footing of an inferior *caste.* This would not probably be the case in our country, at least for one or two generations, and as good conduct is, and ought to be, a *sine qua non*, the innumerable places disposed of by our government might well be committed to the faithful employé qualified to perform his duties, instead, as has been often hitherto the case, of being bestowed, without regard to character and qualification, as a reward for party political services.

But might not such a system be used as a party instrument by unscrupulous politicians? Certainly, and the law should, as far as possible, guard against such a danger. It is clear, however, that the danger of rewarding unworthy party servants with public places would not be increased by such a system,

---

* About *one thousand pensions* are thus provided for per annum They lose their pensions only as they obtain places with the *Scheins* equal to the pension.

but rather narrowed in its operations, and it would be for the wisdom of the legislative power to provide means of counteracting it as far as possible.

While the common soldier and subordinate officer are thus secured from want, the family, after his death, has no legal claim, but private benevolence, under the patronage of the government, has done much for this class in the form of orphan schools and asylum.

The number of pensioned soldiers in 1852 was 29,000, at about the expense of 790,000 thalers. The number has diminished in ten years to 21,000; the expenses to 570,000 thalers.

The law of 1851 does not refer to superior officers. These are of course, in a higher degree, objects of public favor, and the aggregate costs amount to about two millions of thalers. 30 years' service entitles to a pension of half-pay. The highest pension is the whole pay.

* * * * * * *

It may be added that an annual appropriation of 100,000 thalers is given for the relief of families of deceased officers. Such items are accorded as 30 thalers a year for a boy's school-money, and 24 for a girl's. The number of pensioned officers amounts to 4,000, and the aggregate cost 2½ million thalers.*

* * * * * * *

It might be added that the government is quite satisfied with

---

* Number of pensioned soldiers in 1862, 21,000; aggregate amount of annual pensions, Th. 570,125; average pension of soldier per annum, Th. 27 (about $).

Number of pensioned officers in 1862, 4,000; aggregate amount of pensions, Th. 2,788,611; average pension of officers per annum, Th. 697 (about $).

But the disparity in favor of *rank* will more fully appear by comparison with France, where officers forming *one-fifth* of the pension list receive only 15-33 of the pension fund, while in Prussia officers forming less than *one-sixth* of the pension list, receive 25-30 of the fund, or *seventy-five* per cent. more.

RECAPITULATION.

			Cost.	Average Thalers per man.
No. of pensioned soldiers, 1862,	21,000	Th. 570,125	27
" " officers, "	4,000	2,788,611	697
		Th. 3,358,736	

the pension system, but the Chambers have attacked it as too
expensive.

Accompanied by Capt. Von Boehn, I personally visited the
Prussian military invalid hospital in Berlin. We were very
courteously received by Lieutenant Von Gersdorf, one of the
chief employés of the administration of this establishment,
which is under the care of Gen. Malizewski. Every information we required was carefully given. There are no printed
reports. The building is a spacious edifice, surrounded by an
extensive park; the whole founded and presented by Frederick
the Great, and possessing from him a rent of 150,000 thalers,
often increased by legacies, &c. There are 400 occupants, who
suffer no other control than the rule to be in every evening at
9 o'clock. The building and land to-day would probably cost
100,000 thalers. Another hospital for 400 sick, cost the building alone 180,000 thalers. Special accounts could be obtained,
if required. The yearly expenses for food and salary are
42,000 thalers; for keeping up the establishment, warming,
lighting, etc., 12,000 thalers; for clothing, 3,000 thalers. Organized as follows:

1 commandant.
8 chefs de compagnies.
8 first-lieutenants.
9 second-lieutenants.

400 men, of whom a hundred may be married. The pensioners receive gratuitously lodging, washing, cloth, light, fuel,
everything except board and drink. They pay for food out of
their pension one groschen and a quarter a day. They may
drink what, and as much as they like, of course paying for it
themselves. The whole expense of the establishment for food,
salary, clothing, lighting, warming, etc., amounts to 57,000
Prussian thalers a year, exclusive of rent. Fête days, Christmas,
king's birthday, etc., wine and other additions to the fare are
made.

* * * * * * *

I am, sir, with the greatest respect,
Your obedient servant,
THEO. S. FAY.

Berlin, November 21, 1862.
STEPHEN H. PERKINS, Esq.

Extract from second letter of Mr. Fay, *replying to certain inquiries.*

Hospitals.

1. There are but two in Prussia—one in Berlin, with 400 invalids, one in Stolpe, with 80. Both organized in the same way.

2. On entering, invalids lose their pensions. If they wish to leave, they can receive their pensions again, but then they can return no more.

3. The estimate per head, of 160½ thalers, for the 400 men, is incorrect, as the 57,000 thalers, and 180,000 thalers for the building, are not devoted to those 400 men alone. There are, besides them, gratuitously lodged in the building, twenty-six officers, four physicians, and the commandant, a general. These have lodging, fire, service. The officers, often married men, have from three to seven of the best rooms apiece, so that a very considerable deduction must be made.

4. The right to a pension of first class, is by preference accorded to the greatest cripples.

Of Invalid Companies.

5. The same institution as the *invalid houses*, except the tenants have somewhat more freedom. There are seven invalid companies in Prussia, distributed through the provinces. If Prussia had more invalid houses, these companies would not exist. It is neither particularly advantageous nor disadvantageous to be stationed there. The men are quartered upon private families, and make themselves useful, if they wish to do so, and thus earn something. The pension of the first class entitles them to entrance. Nothing is gained, nothing lost, by entering, except they resign their pensions.

6. Without officers and physicians, 600—with officers and physicians, 651.

7. The members lose their pensions, as before stated, and they are not counted among the 25,000 pensioners. The 25,000 comprise 4,000 officers and 21,000 soldiers. Among the officers are counted pensioned physicians and administrative officers.

Of the Reserved Battalion.

8. These questions are answered in my previous letter. The members are soldiers disqualified for field service, but yet qualified for military service at home. They do not belong to the 25,000 pensioners, and receive no pension. They are stationed in fortresses, large cities, etc. They are paid as other soldiers. Their advantage is a lighter service. Each of the eight provinces has one reserved battalion, and each battalion about 500 men ; so the aggregate of 4,000 men.

Of Invalids Provided with the Versorgungs-schein.

9. To your question No. 9, touching the versorgungs-schein, you say that the number of French pensioners is 57,000, of which 46,603 soldiers, and that the French army is twice as large as that of Prussia, and constantly at war. You find, therefore, a great disproportion in 25,000 Prussian pensioners, of whom 21,000 soldiers, when you annually add 1,500 new applicants, provided with versorgungs-schein.

Answer : This disproportion would really exist, if 1,500 versorgungs-schein entitling to places were annually given to new cases, continually added by the small Prussian army in time of peace; which would raise, in ten years, the number of pensioners from 25,000 to 40,000. But this is not the case. The whole number of Prussian pensioners, officers and soldiers, are, with one exception, included in the 25,000. The versorgungs-schein is given to the oldest and most pressing cases among the 25,000 pensioners, and only to such as are entitled to the pension of the first class. Any increase beyond the natural diminution in the number of pensioners, is therefore not to be inferred from the annual issue of so many versorgungs-schein..

The pension is not abandoned on receiving the versorgungs-schein, unless they receive a place equal in value to the pension. In that case, as they receive no further pension, they are not any more counted among the 25,000 pensioners. There must be, of course, a continual succession of individuals among the class of pensioners. There will, as it is composed of the aged and the invalid, be naturally more deaths than in other classes, and the military service, often very severe even in time of peace, will also constantly furnish new contributions. The whole number has decreased.

REMARK.—The versorgungs-schein is not a place—it is only a promise of a place, when a vacancy shall occur. The 1,500 new cases must not annually be added, but undoubtedly to the number of 25,000, as constituting the persons entitled to pen-. sion, must be added such possessors of versorgungs-schein as have received places, and thus abandon their pensions. The question then arises: how many these are? The average is about two-thirds.

10. The king advances whom he likes, without schein, up to captains. The pensions of the higher officers are so high as to render any ordinary office out of the question. The actual sum paid annually by the Prussian government for pensions, is 3,358,736 thalers, of which 2,788,611 thalers for officers, and the rest for common soldiers.

With regard to your closing query, pointing out how much more equitable the government favor appears apportioned between the officers and soldiers in France than in Prussia, it is stated that the principal support extended to higher officers in France, is drawn from the war budget, and not from the pension fund. This, however, seems to me erroneous.

I am, my dear Mr. Perkins,

Very sincerely yours,

THEO. S. FAY.

AUSTRIA.

1st. In the Austrian service pensions are not granted for length of service, or of age, but only to those who, during service, have become by wounds, or otherwise, " unfit for *further service*."

2d. The pension to officers is one-tenth of full pay, if they are pensioned during the first 5 or 10 years service (according to rank) and increases to full pay, as the number of years of active service increases. Officers in hospital (*i. e.*, those who have lost a limb or are blind or epileptic) receive full pay.

3d. Common soldiers not entitled to enter hospital (constituting the vast mass of invalids), receive *five new kreutzers* pension per day, and must take care of themselves. If they have lost a limb they get 10 new kreutzers *additional ;* if they have lost two limbs, or are quite blind, they receive an addition of 20 ` kreutzers a-day, in lieu of ten.

4th. Officers or soldiers are admitted into the Invalid hospitals and "Filialien" *only* when they have lost a limb, or the use of one ; or have received such other wounds as entirely incapacitate them to help themselves, and have no other resource ; or when exceedingly old ; or blind, or deaf, or insane, or epileptic.

5th. When they are admitted into hospital they *retain* their pensions, and are fed and clothed beside.

N.B.—It follows from the above that the *minimum* of the soldiers' pension is 5 kreutzers per diem (say 2¼ cents), and liberty to find work; the *maximum*, 25 kreutzers per diem (11 cents), plus his board and and lodging. The subaltern receive 6 to 20 kreutzers minimum.

6th. The present number of Austrian military pensions is 69,650, amounting last year

to the sum of.........Florins 10,250,025

viz.:

For officers...............	8,590		
Non-combatants...........	2,375	Amount for officers and non-	
Widows & orphans (officers')	6,475	combatants	7,851,165
Soldiers	49,809	Widows and orphans.......	933,870
Out of hospital........	67,249	.	8,785,035
Officers 200		Amount for soldiers in and	
Soldiers............. 2,201		out of hospital..........	1,465,000
In hospital or "filialien"....	2,401	*Pensions,......Florins*	10,250,035
		Cost of three hospitals and	
Total number of pensions	69,650	three filialien............	389,245

Total cost of Invalids............10,639,280

N.B.—An Austrian florin or guilder, contains one hundred new kreutzers, and is equal to, say 45 cents.

7th. There are three invalid hospitals—one at Vienna, one at Pragne, one at Tyrnau, and three "filialien,"* one at Neulerchenfeldt, one at Ciridale, one at Skality—the whole containing 200 officers and 2,201 soldiers, and costing, including salaries of 78 administrative officers: Florins, 389,245 = 162 florins per head.

It appears from this statement that the great part of the pension fund is received here, as in Prussia, by the class of officers, and indeed the common soldier, unless his injuries are of a kind to secure him a place in hospital, is worse off here than in Prussia. The number of pensioned officers is large, being, with the non-combatants and widows, one quarter of the whole number of pensions. The average of officers and non-combatants seems small, viz., about 700 florins a year, that of widows about 144 florins, and that of *all the soldiers and subalterns*, in and out of hospital, 28 *florins per annum* or 7¾ kreutzers, a little over *three cents a day*.

.

---

* The filialien I suppose to be companies analogous to the "Invalid Companies" of Prussia.

In France the minimum is 1 franc a day, say 20 cts. per day.
" Prussia "   "   " 12 thlrs. per an., say $2\frac{1}{2}$ cts.   "
" Austria "   "   " 5 krtzrs. per day, say $2\frac{1}{4}$ cts.   "
In France $\frac{1}{3}$ of pensions, being officers, receive $\frac{15}{33}$ of fund.
" Prussia $\frac{1}{6}$ "   "   "   "   " $\frac{28}{33}$ "
" Austria $\frac{1}{4}$ "   "   including widows " $\frac{23}{33}$ "

The democratic principle has been applied to the subject in France for some years, but has not yet reached Germany.

On the whole I do not see that we can find much to imitate in the Austrian pension or hospital laws.

~~~~~~~~~~~~~~~~~~~~~~

RUSSIA.

Pension System of Russia.[*]

The fundamental idea of this system, is, that, every one in the employment of the State who has served during a certain length of time, (25 years in public schools, 30 years in the medical staff, and 35 years in the military service, and other branches of the Government,) retires with a pension equal to the compensation of his last office.

After death, one-half of this pension passes to his widow, who enjoys it during life, or until her second marriage, the other half is divided among his children during their minority. There are cases in which a right to a pension arises before quitting the service, which is equivalent to a double compensation.

Should the person retire from service after from 15 to 25 years, he receives a pension equal to one-half of the pay of his last office. At his death one-half goes to his widow, the other to his children. But if, during his term of service, the person is attacked by any disease, however indirectly it may have been produced by the labors or duties of his office, or if he has met with an accident, occurring during such service, he has a right to be retired with a pension of from 5 to 10 years in advance of

---

his lawful time. That is to say, that a disease produced by the duties of the service, or occurring to a person while in service, diminishes, according to the degree of its severity, by 5 or 10 years, the legal time required by law to earn a pension. Wounds, in soldiers, also give a right to a pension, in advance of the required term of service. Of these there are three classes:

1st. Such as, at any moment, give a right of retiring with a pension.

2d. Such as diminish the legal time by 10 years, and

3d. Such as diminish the legal time by 5 years.

With the exception of these general regulations, there exists in Russia a subordinate pension fund for wounded men, founded by the Emperor Alexander 1st, in 1815, under the name of " Committee on the Wounded." Disposing of large sums, it allots pensions to the wounded, independently of ordinary pensions.

During the year 1862, the amount of pensions paid reached as high as 10,000,000 roubles.

The per diem of expense for invalids in hospital varies from 35 to 75 copeks.

ITALY.

PENSIONS.

1st. The Italian Government grants military pensions " *de re-traitcs*" (*a*) for length of service, of thirty years to commissioned officers, and of twenty-five years to subalterns and soldiers, (*b*) for injuries and disease incurred in service.

2d. All those who receive pensions are stricken off the army list, and re-enter civil life.

3d. Those pensioned for length of service receive the minimum rate ; but if they have served longer than the required time, the rate rises with the excess of service till it reaches the maximum.

4th. Those pensioned for injuries receive the pension whatever the time of service ; when they have become blind, or lost two limbs, they receive the maximum increased 50 per cent. If the injury is equal to the loss of one limb, they receive the maximum. For any lesser injury, the minimum.

5th. Widows and orphans left by those dying from injuries, receive half the maximum. If the death occur while in receipt of a pension, but not from injuries received in war, the widow, &c., gets one-quarter of the pension.

6th. The tariff allows—

	Max.	Min.
For a General of Division	8,000	6,000
" Colonel	3,600	2,700
Captain	1,900	1,400
Soldier	350	200

francs or livres per annum.

7th. { Total number of "militaires retraités" 30,229
1863 { Total amount of pensions .... Frs. 15,748,328
Proportion of officers and their pensions not given.

HOSPITALS FOR VETERANS AND INVALIDS.

1st. There are now two in Italy called Case Reale.

One at *Asti* containing inmates............ 2,431

"   " *Naples*........................ .. 8,148

10,579

each under command of a major-general with a regular staff.

2d. Cost of both estimated for 1863, francs 6,388,593.

3d. They contain two distinct corps (*a*) *veterans*, viz., those unfit for active but capable of garrison service, &c., (*b*) *Invalids* who are unfit for any service.

4th. Although only the first are armed, they are both classed as soldiers, and as such do not receive *pensions*, but have special allowances in money and rations, from which they pay their own expenses. The Government, however, furnishes the subalterns and soldiers with food, clothes, bed, and fire, to cover which, certain sums are retained from the pay, as detailed in the report, and the balance is paid them in cash. After being so provided for, there seems to be about three francs per month paid to the common soldier—equal to about one week's wages for a common laborer.

5th. In these houses there are two kinds of schools with paid teachers, viz., (*a*) one for boys learning music to join the army bands, (*b*) one for children of the soldiers of both sexes, where reading, writing, arithmetic, &c., are taught. Special appropriations are made for the expense of these schools, for the arms of the veterans, hospital expenses, &c., all being comprised in the above aggregate.

6th. The veterans are drafted off into three kinds of service, (*a*) into garrisons in the proportion of one-fifth of garrison, (*b*) into the guards of the royal palaces, (*c*) into the gendarmerie in the proportion of one-fourth of latter. The gendarme recruits are from subalterns. They are also employed as scribes, porters, and servants.

7th. The allowance to veterans and invalids is higher to the officers than the maximum, and higher to the soldier than the minimum pensions, viz.:

To a colonel it is frs. 6,600, to a captain frs. 2,200, and to a soldier 80 centimes per diem, say 292 frs. per annum.

8th. Total number of pensioners, invalids, and
    veterans...................... 40,808
Total cost of military pensions and hospitals for
    invalids and veterans.................. frs. 22,136,921

9th. Average per head per annum, together.. " 542½
    Do.   "   "   "   " pensions.... " 521
    Do.   "   "   "   " invalids, &c. " 603

N. B.—The Government is about to establish a first class invalid hospital in the Poggio Imperiale, near the Roman gate of Florence.

I regret that the government did not furnish a statement of the proportion of the pension money paid to officers and widows. As regards the invalid hospitals, they appear to have been established on an extravagant basis, as compared with the pensions.

This is so everywhere, for one reason or another, but nowhere so much as in Italy. There seems to have been good feeling shown in the construction of those laws, and there are some great improvements on the French practice, such as the introduction of schools, the employment of those capable of labor (the veterans), &c., but, on the other hand, there is great want of judgment shown in making the condition of the common soldier in hospital too attractive, and so stimulating the national fault of lack of independence and energy. The consequence is, that the number of those in hospital is one-third as large as the whole number of pensioners, and the cost of maintaining them, including the schools, over two-fifths of the pensions. In France, where the right to enter the hospital is very much the same, the number of pensioners is 57,366, and the number in hospital only 2,099, which shows a difference very honorable to French character. The cost per head, in hospital in France, is so high because the hotel is fitted and officered for double the number it contains, but here the hospitals are crowded (that of Naples must be a monster establishment), and the great cost per head is owing to an excessive allowance to the officers and soldiers in hospital. This I consider one of the greatest faults which can be made in establishing a hospital system, though its effect in America or France would probably not be so apparent as in Italy. The Italians will, however, probably rather increase than diminish the faults in new establishments.

www.ingramcontent.com/pod-product-compliance
Lightning Source LLC
Chambersburg PA
CBHW022039080426
42733CB00007B/901